AT HIS FEET

By Sherry Long
Digging a Well Ministries

Website
https://diggingawell.org

Blog
https://diggingawell.blogspot.com

Copyright © 2024 Sherry Long
All rights reserved. No part of this book may be reproduced or transmitted in any form or by any means, electronic or mechanical, including photocopying, recording or by any information storage and retrieval system, without permission in writing from the copyright owner.

This book was printed in the United States of America.

TABLE OF CONTENTS

GOD THE FATHER	5

GOD THE SON	14

GOD THE HOLY SPIRIT	24

GOD THE FATHER

Genesis 1:1, "In the beginning!"

How many times have you read those words?

"In the beginning God!"

Did that change the way you thought about Genesis 1:1, just by adding one more word?

"In the beginning, God created the heavens and the earth!"

Consider this thought and write down what those words truly mean.

How did He create the heavens and earth?

Did He use a magic wand?

Did He say Abracadabra?

Did He snap his finger?

No.

It was the spoken word! The very breath of God! We could go off on a complete study on the word "breath," but that is not what this book is about. We could also go off on a complete study on the word "Word" but that still is not what this book is about. This book is about *the very presence of God* coming to stand before us, and thus allowing us to come and stand before His presence.

When He finished creating the heavens and the earth, something seemed to be missing. On the sixth day, He bent down, picked up dust, and formed that heap of dust into His very image.

Do you think He stopped and contemplated for a moment? Silly clay, we can put a dimple here, how about a small wart, maybe two noses. What if we design him with one arm here and a leg on the other side of his chest? What if we shorten one leg so that when this man I created walks, I could sit in the great heaven and chuckle a bit at his awkwardness.

No, He knew He wanted this man to be perfect, made in His image.

There it is, a little clay figure right before God's eyes. That is all it was, just a clay figure.

Now what?

We can dwell on this thought for a while, but as a Facility Lead heading up the First Aid Team at my office, I understand what it takes to revive a human being once they lose consciousness. It takes putting my mouth to their mouth and breathing my breath into their lungs. Suddenly the person comes around and has a pulse once again.

God had already created the heavens and the earth, by His very words breathed out. He breathed out and His words turned the sky blue, the ocean was filled with water, and the trees were filled with fruits, nuts, birds, bugs, and the creations kept coming.

When He created mankind, it was different. He took His own breath and placed it inside of mankind and new life, human life sprang forth for the very first time.

He did not form mankind like all His other creations. Yes, they were filled with splendor and majesty, but He took this clay figure a step further. He placed His feet right on top of the very dust mankind would walk on. He bent down and touched the dust, He formed the dust, and He breathed life into this lump of dust.

Yet, He still was not finished! He also formed the woman, not quite like the man, but so similar.

Women are created uniquely for a reason. This also could be another whole study, but we understand why God wanted women to be different. A little diamond nugget shining among the clay. Unique, delicate, tender, sweet, and filled with something slightly different from the man, just enough difference to make the man scratch his head and ponder. Never quite figuring the woman out, yet loving her with a depth that could not be explained.

Read John 1: 1-14 and try to figure out those first few verses.

If you can figure them out you are serving a small god. He would not be our Great Almighty God.

God is so far beyond our imagination and ability to explain.

Why?

Because: He is God!

John 1:1-14
Vs. 1 In the beginning was the Word, and the Word was with God, and the Word was God.

Vs. 2 The same was in the beginning with God.

Vs. 3 All things were made by Him and, without Him was not anything made that was made.

Vs. 4 In Him was life; and the life was the light of men.

Vs. 5 And the light shineth in darkness; and the darkness comprehended it not.

Vs. 6 There was a man sent from God, whose name was John.

Vs. 7 The same came for a witness, to bear witness of the Light, that all men through Him might believe.

Vs. 8 He was not that Light, but was sent to bear witness of that Light.

Vs. 9 That was the true Light, which lighteth every man that cometh into the world.

Vs. 10 He was in the world, and the world was made by Him, and the world knew Him not.

Vs. 11 He came unto His own, and His own received Him not.

Vs. 12 But as many as received Him, to them gave He power to become the sons of God, even to them that believe on His name:

Vs. 13 Which were born, not of blood, nor of the will of the flesh, nor of the will of man, but of God.

Vs. 14 And the Word was made flesh, and dwelt among us, (and we beheld his glory as of the only begotten of the Father,) full of grace and truth.

Write down on paper why you feel God the Father wanted to be present when creating mankind. Why He wanted the personal touch of His hand upon His creation.

Discuss why He wanted His breath to bring forth human life, instead of the spoken word; as with the creation of the heavens and earth.

NOTES

NOTES

NOTES

GOD THE SON

The blood dripping from His body, hitting His feet as He walks up the lonely dusty road.

Lonely road?

Maybe that would be the thought running through some minds; the road is filled with people who had days before lined the streets, waved palm leaves, and cried, "Hosanna" in front of this man they call Jesus.

How could it be so very lonely now?

Before Christ walked the road to Golgotha, the people in the city were in an uproar. They began to accuse the disciples of being Jesus' followers.

> Mark 14:67-68
> *When she saw Peter warming himself, she looked closely at him. "You also were with Jesus of Nazareth" she said. But He denied it, saying, "I neither know nor understand what you are talking about." And He went out onto the porch, and a rooster crowed.*

Out of fear, one by one they hid away or began to watch from a distance.

When the cross became too heavy to bear; where were the disciples that had spent every day, learning at His feet?

The five thousand who had witnessed the breaking of the bread, where had they gone?

Where were the people whose thirst He quenched now? Where were the people that were healed, the ones raised from the dead, the wedding party that received the best quality wine ever, those receiving food to eat while standing at the feet of Jesus? Where had they all gone?

Reaching the top of the hill where the final crucifixions would take place, Jesus realized this was a path that no other would walk with Him.

Innocent, yet proven guilty by the mob.

Despised, rejected, beaten to a bloody pulp, waiting to receive the cruelest death of all times, yet not one of the disciples or followers was there to be of support.

Think back to the loneliest time in your life and write down the emotions you felt.

Do you think they compare to how Christ was feeling at this time?

Write down the ways your emotions compared to Jesus' emotions.

Write down how your emotions differed from Jesus' emotions, at this point in His life. As Mary was standing at the foot of the cross, how do you think she viewed life at this moment?

Thinking back, Mary remembered the moment the Savior was born. She had softly rubbed her hands over His gentle tiny hands and feet, feeling with awe the wonder of this newborn child, the Savior of the world.

How can this be?

The Christ-child there in her arms, what if she messed this whole thing up?

What if she messed it up so badly that He was crucified instead of becoming the King?

Would it be the fact that she had accidentally left Jesus at the temple at the age of twelve and He was never able to overcome the scars?

Would it be the fact that Jesus was not ready to display His glory at the wedding and she pleaded for Him to fix the situation?

How could she possibly teach the Savior of the world the needed skills?

Would she succeed or would she fail?

Suddenly, she was jolted back to reality as the soldiers grabbed Jesus up, not gently, but with force. They laid Jesus on the cross, picked up the old nails and began to hammer His body to the cross.

These were no small nails. Some say they could have been seven inches long, and I'm sure they were plenty thick. They had to be long enough to pierce through both feet. The soldier placed one foot on top of the other foot, the other soldier picking up the nail and hammer. The soldiers thought they were finalizing His death. God realized they were nailing down something far greater than His body. The final decree was being nailed down, signed, and delivered to all generations, "This is the Christ, the Son of the Living God."

This decree could not be altered in any way, as it was a blood decree.

As Mary watched her Son hanging there, pushing up on His feet to gather enough air to hang on a little longer, she must have pondered over the events of His life, once again.

"God, what is going on?"

"Did you not send your angel to tell Joseph this baby would be the Savior of the world? "

"Did the shepherds not hear the multitude of angels singing, "Glory to God in the highest, peace goodwill to all men?" Luke2:14

Did the angel not come to Mary herself and deliver the good news that she would give birth to the Savior of the World?

"Is this what you call peace? "

The baby born in a manger had lain there so sweetly. As she looked at His feet then and looked at His feet now, she must have certainly been confused.

Oh God! How I failed to raise the Savior of the World!

Now what?

He had grown up with all the other boys, played games the same as they did, combed His hair the same, slept the same hours, and attended the same schools. He was much the same, yet so different. Maybe if she had forced Him to be different, to stand out amongst the crowd, to walk with pride and arrogance instead of humility.

Too late! It is too late!

Then she pondered once more.

It was not until He was in His 30's that He had begun to perform miracles. Still, He walked the same dusty roads, wore the same fabric of clothing, and talked the same as all the other men.

At His feet men were healed of blindness, women healed of infirmities.

Those tiny feet she once held in her hands, provided shoes for, and washed gently were now being nailed to the cruel cross. Great confusion was taking place in the heart of Mary. How could He be King of Kings and Lord of Lords, if He was going to die?

Then, days later, the story suddenly began to unfold.

He arose! Those feet still bore the scars of Calvary, reminding Mary just why it was that God sent His Son.

He ascended! His feet touched the Mount of Olives, He began His ascent upward.

His promise to return – His feet will once again touch the Mount of Olives.

"All this is happening so quickly. I must trust that God is still fulfilling a greater plan."

NOTES

NOTES

NOTES

GOD THE HOLY SPIRIT

Mary must have said, "Alright God! I have missed all these things that came before me to this moment, how am I going to understand this prophecy that You are sending the Holy Spirit?"

Ever feel like Mary?

Jesus did not hang around to explain. They would soon figure it out.

> *Acts 1:6-12*
> *Vs. 6 When they therefore were come together, they asked of Him, saying, Lord, wilt thou at this time restore again the kingdom to Israel?*
>
> *Vs. 7 And He said unto them, It is not for you to know the times or the seasons, which the Father hath put in His own power.*
>
> *Vs. 8 But ye shall receive power, after that the Holy Ghost is come upon you: and ye shall be witnesses unto me both in Jerusalem, and in all Judea, and in Samaria, and unto the uttermost part of the earth.*
>
> *Vs. 9 And when He had spoken these things, while they beheld, He was taken up; and a cloud received Him out of their sight.*

Vs. 10 And while they looked steadfastly toward heaven as He went up, behold, two men stood by them in white apparel;

Vs. 11 Which also said, Ye men of Galilee, why stand ye gazing up into heaven? this same Jesus, which is taken up from you into heaven, shall so come in like manner as ye have seen Him go into heaven.

Vs. 12 Then returned they unto Jerusalem from the mount called Olivet, which is from Jerusalem a sabbath day's journey.

Jesus ascended upward into Heaven. Verse ten states, they looked steadfastly, as He went up." I am sure their mouths were wide open as they gazed, until the last thing they saw was Jesus' feet.

The two angels standing on the sideline said, "Get ready; do not stand around here, because just as Jesus ascended into Heaven, He will surely return the same way."

Jesus had completed His earthly journey and now understood what we (mankind) needed.
He understood our need to have someone live among us, yet He was leaving.

He comprehended our need to wake up daily knowing He had taken our guilt from us by His crucifixion, but in place of the guilt, He had left a Comforter. Not a comforter for your bed, but one for your heart. Something you can grab hold of, and hang on to through the birth of a child, sicknesses, and even death.

Jesus told them in John 16:7-8 "Nevertheless I tell you the truth; It is expedient for you that I go away: for if I go not away, the Comforter will not come unto you; but if I depart, I will send Him unto you."

Never left alone again but always having the Holy Spirit, another part of the Godhead, as a guide for their lives, and now for our lives.

Will you still experience the new life of a baby being born, tragedies, sickness, and death once this comforter arrives?

Yes, but you will never experience these events alone.

The Holy Spirit will be with you to help you cope. All you need to do to keep warm physically is reach for a comforter. All you need to do to keep warm spiritually is, reach for "The Comforter, Jesus Christ."

His presence is there, we must reach out to Him, so He can draw near to us.

Do not ask Him to only be there long enough to wipe your nose and eyes on after a long cry, over your hurts, your sins, or your past. But, to truly draw Him in, hold Him close and allow His peace to flow over your wounded heart, not just today, but forever.

You must let go and allow the Holy Spirit to have control of your heart, mind, and soul.

You may say, "I gave Him my soul!" but that is not enough.

"OK, well I gave Him my heart and soul!"

That still is not enough!

You must give Him your heart to move you in a new direction. But, if you give Him your heart only, what is going to keep you moving in that right direction?

Ah, it is your mind!

You must set your heart and mind on the same path God intends for you.

Jeremiah 17:9 The heart is deceitful above all things, and desperately wicked: who can know it?

Proverbs 4:23 Keep thy heart with all diligence; for out of it are the issues of life.

Matthew 22:37 Jesus said unto Him, Thou shalt love the Lord thy God with all thy heart, and with all thy soul, and with all thy mind.

Luke 10:27 And He answering said, Thou shalt love the Lord thy God with all thy heart, and with all thy soul, and with all thy strength, and with all thy mind; and love thy neighbor as thyself.

If you get your heart and your mind moving in the same direction, your soul is going to follow.

If you set your mind but not your heart, your heart will get off the trail chasing a squirrel.

If you set your heart in the right direction, your mind, not being under control, can instantly wander down a path of destruction and along with it, the soul will follow.

Therefore, we must set aside time to readjust our thinking habits. We must also set our hearts on removing obstacles that would be a distraction.

In addition, we need to take time to get into the Word and focus on the Lord.

Setting your heart and soul in the same direction is like watching the soldiers at the tomb of the Unknown Soldier. Rain can be falling; they do not flinch. A beautiful lady can pass by; they do not flinch. A child can set off a firecracker, they do not flinch. The soldier's heart and mind are set. It is locked and there is no unlocking it for food, water, or pleasure, until the moment the soldier is off-duty.

What are some areas you have experienced having your mind set and found your heart led you astray?

What are some areas you have experienced having your heart set and suddenly your mind was the one to lead you astray?

Can you see the importance of the heart and mind being on the same path?

This book's intent has been to help you to see the importance of God walking among us from the beginning of time, throughout this earthly life and all the way into life eternal.

Jesus lived among mankind, touching the same soil we walk on. His feet experiencing the same feelings we experience daily, whether it is God the Father, God the Son, or God the Holy Spirit.

The depth of God the Father, God the Son, and God the Holy Spirit, is so vital in our Christian Walk. If we learn to trust each of these entities of the God Head, our destination will be, the eternal walk, when God opens the gates of heaven, and welcomes us in.

A place where not only His feet had walked, but you will find your place at His feet, just as the title of this book states.

I do not know what that moment will be like. I can only imagine seeing Him face to face. Eyes fixed on no other and hearing His voice for the first time as the Lord God says, "Welcome my good and faithful servant, you may enter the kingdom of God."

This God who spoke the words and instantly the galaxies began to glisten and orbit in perfect time has just looked me in the eye and welcomed me to spend eternity in a spectacular kingdom above with streets of gold and gates of pearl.

The Lord is doing this, not because I deserve it. He is doing it because of His great love and compassion for a little lump of clay. The clay He once bent down, created, and held onto so dearly, never letting go of and offering forgiveness, grace and hope for life eternal.

Let us take time to prepare our hearts, minds & souls for that day! The day of the Lord!

NOTES

NOTES

NOTES

Made in the USA
Middletown, DE
12 January 2025